PIANO SOLO

THE CHARLIE BROWN COLLECTION™

CONTENTS

ISBN 0-634-03084-1

HAL•LEONARD®
CORPORATION

7777 W. BLUEMOUND RD. P.O. BOX 13819 MILWAUKEE, WI 53213

PEANUTS © United Feature Syndicate, Inc.
www.snoopy.com

Visit Hal Leonard Online at
www.halleonard.com

BASEBALL THEME

CHRISTMAS IS COMING

PEANUTS © United Feature Syndicate, Inc.

CHRISTMAS TIME IS HERE

THE GREAT PUMPKIN WALTZ

LINUS
AND LUCY

RED BARON

SCHROEDER

SKATING

CHARLIE BROWN THEME

By VINCE GUARALDI

BASEBALL THEME

By VINCE GUARALDI

Moderate Jazz Waltz

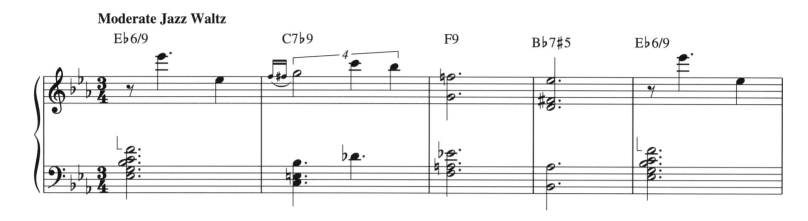

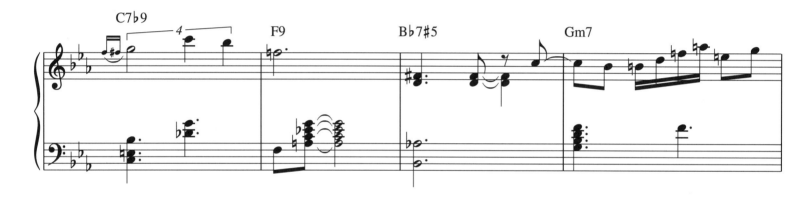

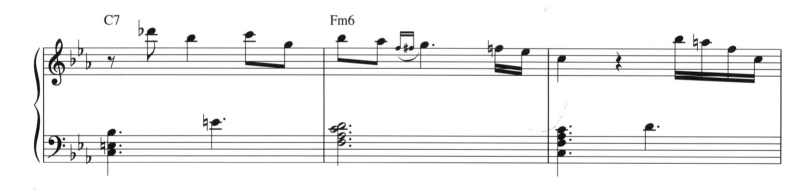

BLUE CHARLIE BROWN

By VINCE GUARALDI

CHRISTMAS IS COMING

By VINCE GUARALDI

Bright Bossa, Rock feel

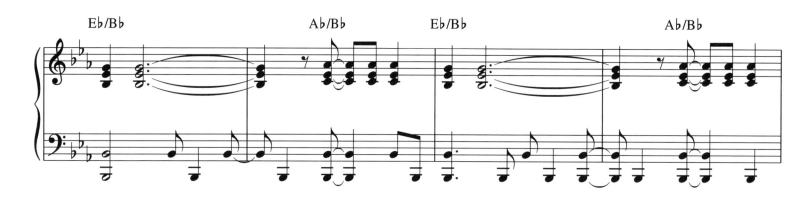

21

CHRISTMAS TIME IS HERE

Words by LEE MENDELSON
Music by VINCE GUARALDI

Christ - mas time is here, hap - pi - ness and
Snow - flakes in the air, car - ols ev - 'ry -

cheer. Fun for all that chil - dren call their
where. Old - en times and an - cient rhymes of

fa - v'rite time of year.
love and dreams to share.

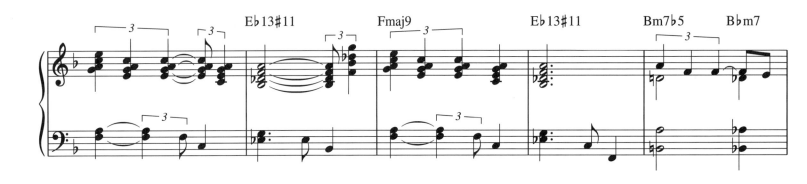

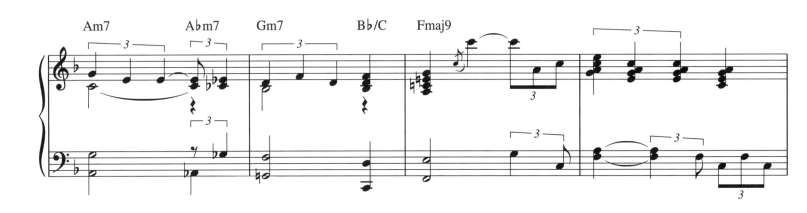

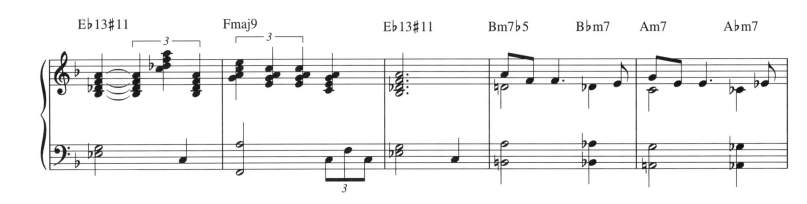

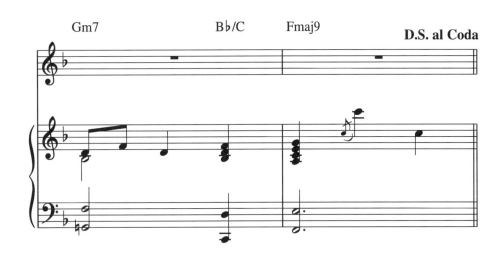

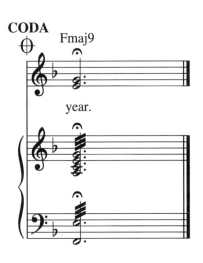

THE GREAT PUMPKIN WALTZ

By VINCE GUARALDI

HAPPINESS THEME

By VINCE GUARALDI

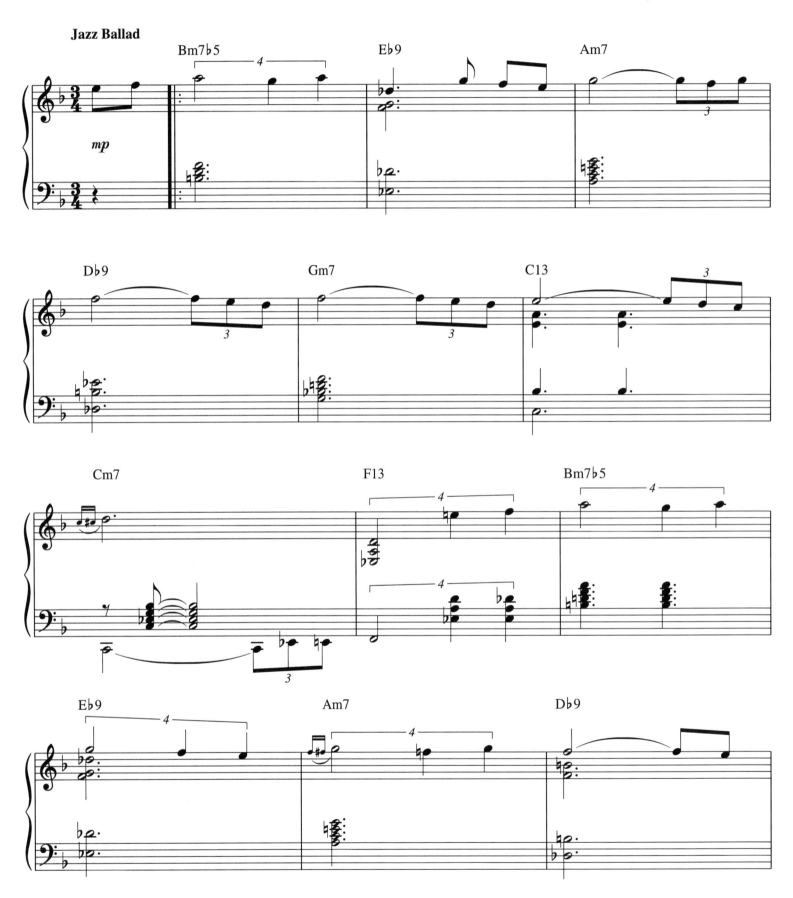

OH, GOOD GRIEF

By VINCE GUARALDI

HE'S YOUR DOG, CHARLIE BROWN

By VINCE GUARALDI

JOE COOL

By VINCE GUARALDI

Moderate Swing

LINUS AND LUCY

By VINCE GUARALDI

LOVE WILL COME

By VINCE GUARALDI

PEPPERMINT PATTY

By VINCE GUARALDI

RAIN, RAIN, GO AWAY

By VINCE GUARALDI

RED BARON

By VINCE GUARALDI

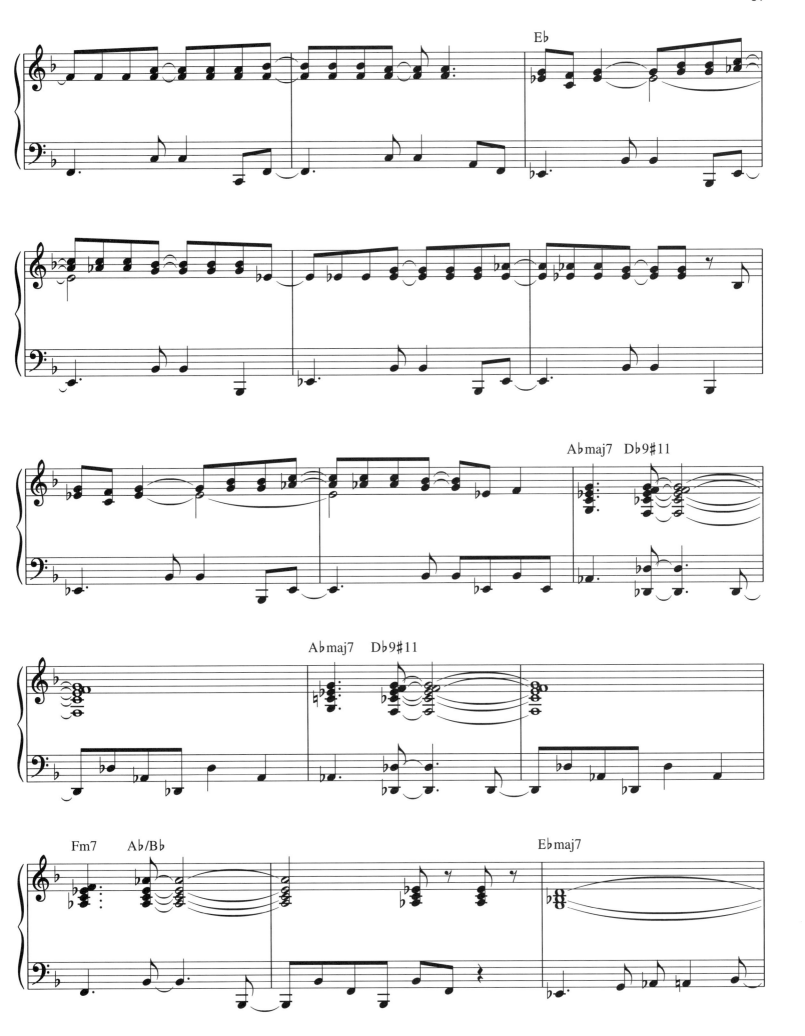

SCHROEDER

By VINCE GUARALDI

Rubato (with motion)

YOU'RE IN LOVE, CHARLIE BROWN

By VINCE GUARALDI

Moderate Jazz Waltz

SKATING

By VINCE GUARALDI

Bright Jazz Waltz

63